LONDON BRIDGE TO ADDISCOMBE

Vic Mitchell and Keith Smith

MP Middleton Press

Cover picture: Woodside was still a junction when the 6.31 pm Cannon Street to Addiscombe was recorded on 19th July 1951. By then the original wooden bodied 3-car sets had been augmented by a wider all-steel coach. (Pamlin Prints)

First published September 1993

ISBN 1 873793 20 0

Design - Deborah Goodridge
Typesetting - Barbara Mitchell
            Deborah Goodridge

Published by Middleton Press
            Easebourne Lane
            Midhurst
            West Sussex
            GU29 9AZ
            Tel: (0730) 813169
(From 16 April 1995 - (01730) 813169)

Printed & bound by Biddles Ltd,
            Guildford and Kings Lynn

CONTENTS

107	Addiscombe
40	Catford Bridge
59	Clock House
120	Croydon Tramlink
77	Eden Park
66	Elmers End
87	Hayes
36	Ladywell
29	Lewisham area
1	London Bridge
47	Lower Sydenham
53	New Beckenham
20	New Cross
18	Spa Road
25	St. Johns
82	West Wickham
96	Woodside

ACKNOWLEDGEMENTS

We are very grateful for the assistance given by many of the photographers mentioned in the credits and for help received from R.M.Casserley, Dr.E.Course, G.Croughton, J.B.Horne, J.R.W.Kirkby, N.Langridge, A.Ll.Lambert, D.Lovett (NSE), A.Neale, D.Pocock, R.Randell, Mr D. and Dr. S. Salter, N.Stanyon and our patient helpful wives.

1955 map

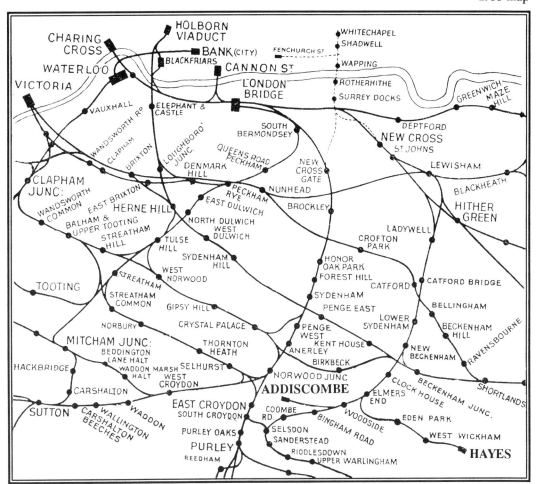

GEOGRAPHICAL SETTING

The route is in the lower Thames Valley as far as Lewisham where it turns south to follow the Ravensbourne River as far as Catford, the Pool River to Beckenham and the Chaffinch Brook south thereof. The termini are situated on the gravels at the foot of the dip slope of the North Downs, Addiscombe being at 180 ft above sea level and Hayes at 200 ft.

Like the Mid-Sussex, the Mid-Kent line was misnamed, both being at the western extremities of their counties. Although boundaries have altered slightly, for most of the life of the route only the New Beckenham-Elmers End section and the Hayes branch have been in Kent.

All maps are to the scale of 25" to 1 mile unless otherwise shown.

HISTORICAL BACKGROUND

The first part of our journey is over the route of the London & Greenwich Railway which opened between Spa Road and Deptford on 8th February 1836, extension to London Bridge taking place on 14th December of that year. The South Eastern Railway leased this venture in 1845.

Trains of the London & Brighton Railway started to use part of this route to London Bridge in 1839, their line via Croydon becoming part of the London, Brighton & South Coast Railway in 1846.

The SER was unable to extend its Greenwich line direct to Woolwich and so constructed a route via Lewisham which opened on 30th July 1849.

The Mid-Kent Railway from Lewisham via Lower Sydenham to Beckenham (now Beckenham Junction) came into use on 1st January 1857 and was worked by the SER. It was Beckenham's first railway, the London Chatham & Dover Railway's east-west route not opening until 3rd May 1858.

The Mid-Kent was extended to Croydon (Addiscombe Road) on 1st April 1864, breaking the LBSCR's monopoly of Croydon traffic. An agreement had been made in 1863 for the SER to acquire control of the Mid-Kent.

The Hayes branch was opened by the SER on 29th May 1882. There followed a joint line with the LBSCR between Woodside and Selsdon on 10th August 1885. This linked the Mid-Kent route with the South Croydon-East Grinstead line which had been opened to traffic on 10th March 1884 and was a joint operation in part.

Electrification of the Hayes branch slightly preceded the remainder of the route. Short electric trains were run on the branch from 21st September 1925, the Charing Cross/Cannon Street to Addiscombe electric service commencing on 28th February 1926. The Woodside-Sanderstead section was electrically operated from 30th September 1935, having been closed to passengers since wartime curtailment of service on 1st January 1917. Total closure of this section took place on 13th May 1983.

Bradshaw January 1857

PASSENGER SERVICES

Reference to the table of sample years gives
an indication of the number of trains per day
on each of the terminal sections.

	Beckenham Junc.		Addiscombe		Hayes		Selsdon	
	Weekdays	Sundays	Weekdays	Sundays	Weekdays	Sundays	Weekdays	Sundays
1857	11	5	-	-	-	-	-	-
1869	18	6	19	4	-	-	-	-
1890	22	6	21	4	13	4	9	-
1911	31	14	34	13	17	10	20	-
1924	11	-	38	15	21	12	-	-
1936	7	-	59	32	58	34	33	32

Note the steady decline in the Beckenham Junction branch and variation on the Selsdon section.

The optimum service of electric trains gave an off-peak frequency of four trains per hour north of Elmers End but this was reduced to three on 13th September 1958 when the Addiscombe shuttle reduced to hourly. The latter was restored to three per hour in the following November when the Sanderstead service was curtailed during the middle of the day, early on Saturdays and totally on Sundays.

Off peak, all trains ran to Hayes from 26th September 1949, Addiscombe and Selsdon/Sanderstead being served by branch trains.

The basic service was reduced to half-hourly from 11th June 1963 but restored to three per hour on 3rd May 1976, but through peak hour working to Addiscombe and Sanderstead ceased almost completely at that time.

Reversion to a half-hour off-peak interval occurred on 16th May 1983.

Bradshaw June 1869

Bradshaw November 1911 down trains

LONDON, NEW BECKENHAM, HAYES, CROYDON, and BECKENHAM JUNCTION.

South Eastern and Chatham.

Week Days.

Miles.	Down.	mrn	mrn	mrn	mrn	mrn	mrn	mrn	mrn	mrn	aft	aft	aft	aft	aft	aft	aft	aft	aft	aft	aft	aft	aft	aft
	Charing Cross..dep.	....	....	....	....	....	....	....	....	1117	1210	1217	12s37	12e48	....	....	....	....	1e28	1s40	....	....	2e12	....
¾	Waterloo Junction.	....	....	....	....	....	....	....	....	1119	1212	1219	12s39	12e50	....	....	....	....	1e30	1s42	....	....	2e14	....
—	Cannon Street	5 41	6 22	713	750	8 0	8 58	9 33	1023	1126	....	1227	12s47	12e57	1 6	1s18	1 23	1 34	1e37	....	2 6	2s16	2e21	2s30
1¾	London Bridge	5 44	6 25	716	753	8 3	9 1	9 36	1026	1129	1217	1230	12s50	1e0	1 9	1s21	1 26	1 37	1e40	1s50	2 9	2s19	2e24	2s33
5	New Cross..........	5 52	6 35	723	8 1	...	9 8	9 43	1035	1136	....	....	12s58	1e7	....	....	1 33	1 45	....	1s57	....	2s26	2e31	....
5½	St. John's	5 55	6 38	...	8 4	...	9 11	9 46	1038	1139	....	....	1s1	1e10	....	....	1 36	1 48	....	2s0	....	....	2e34	....
6	Lewisham Junction	5 58	6 41	...	8 7	813	9 14	9 49	1041	1142	....	....	1s4	1e13	....	....	1 39	1 51	1e50	2s3	2 19	2s30	2e37	....
6¾	Lady Well..........	6 1	6 44	729	...	816	9 17	9 52	1044	1145	1228	1241	1s7	1e16	1 20	1s32	1 42	1 54	1e53	2s6	2 22	2s33	2e40	2s44
7½	Catford Bridge	6 5	6 48	732	812	820	9 21	9 56	1048	1148	1231	1244	1s11	1e19	1 24	1s36	1 46	1 58	1e56	2s10	2 26	2s37	2e43	2s47
9	Lower Sydenham...	6 9	6 52	736	816	...	....	10 0	1052	1152	....	....	1s15	1e23	Saturdays only.	1s40	....	....	....	2s14	....	2s41	2e47	2s51
9¾	New Beckenham ...	6 12	6 55	738	818	825	9 26	10 3	1055	1155	....	....	1s18	1e26		1s43	....	2 3	....	2s17	2 31	2s44	2e50	....
10½	Clock House.......	6 15	6 58	741	821	828	9 30	10 7	1059	1158	1237	1250	1s22	1e29		1s46	1 52	2 6	2e2	2s21	2 34	2s48	2e53	2s55
11	Elmer's End.......	6 18	7 1	744	824	...	9 33	1011	11 2	12 1	Except Sats.	Sats. only.	1s25	1e32		1s49	Sats. only.	Sats. only.	....	2s24	Sats. only.	2s51	2e56	2s58
—	Elmer's End dep.	....	7 6	...	835	...	9 36	1018	1117	....			1s28	1e34		1s54			....	2s30		....	2e58	3s0
12½	Eden Park	....	....	...	839	...	9 40	1022	1121	....			1s32	1e38		1s58			....	2s34		....	3e2	3s4
13¼	West Wickham.	....	7 11	...	842	...	9 43	1025	1124	....			1s35	1e41		2s1			....	2s37		....	3e5	3s7
14½	Hayes..... arr.	....	7 15	...	846	...	9 47	1029	1128	....			1s39	1e45		2s5			....	2s41		....	3e9	3s11
12¼	Woodside ‡ (below)	6 22	7 5	748	...	832	9 36	1015	11 6	12 5	1242	1256	1s29	1e36	1 34	1s53	1 57	2 11	2e7	2s28	2 39	2s55	3e0	3s2
13	Croydon * .... arr.	6 25	7 8	751	829	835	9 39	1018	11 9	12 8	1245	1259	1s32	1e39	1 37	1s56	....	2 14	2e10	2s31	2 42	2s58	3e3	3s5
10¼	Beckenham Jn. "	6 18	7 5	751	...	840	9 38	1010	11 2	12 3	....	....	1s25	1e32	....	1s53	....	2 8	....	2s24	2 39	2s51	2e56	....

Week Days—*Continued.*

Down.	aft	aft	aft	aft	aft	aft	aft	aft	aft	aft	aft	aft	aft	aft	aft	aft	aft	aft	aft	aft	aft	aft	aft	aft
Charing Cross..dep.	....	2s49	2e55	....	....	....	....	....	4s46	....	....	5 17	....	5e50	5s52	....	....	....	....	....	6e45	7s0	....	....
Waterloo Junction.	....	2s51	2e57	....	....	....	....	....	4s48	....	....	5 19	....	5e52	5s54	....	....	....	....	....	6e47	7s2	....	....
Cannon Street	2 46	....	3e4	3s20	3 55	4 8	4 25	4 55	4s55	5 10	5e17	5 26	5 50	5e59	6s1	6 9	6 27	6s27	6 39	6 50	6e54	7s10	7 21	7 40
London Bridge	2 49	2s57	3e7	3s23	3 58	4 11	4 28	4 58	4s58	5 13	5e20	5 29	5 53	6e2	6s4	6 12	6 30	6s30	6 42	6 53	6e57	7s13	7 24	7 43
New Cross..........	2 57	3s4	3e15	3s30	4 5	Except Saturdays.	....	....	5s5	....	5e27	5s35	....	....	....	6 19	....	6s37	6 49	....	....	7s20	7 31	....
St. John's	....	3s7	3e18	3s33	....		....	....	5s8	....	....	....	....	....	....	....	....	6s40	....	....	....	....	....	....
Lewisham Junction	....	3s10	3e21	3s36	4 9		....	....	5s11	....	5e31	....	....	....	6s14	....	6 39	6s43	....	....	....	7s24	7 35	7 52
Lady Well..........	3 4	3s13	3e24	3s39	4 12		4 39	5 9	5s14	5 24	5e34	5 40	6 5	6e13	6s17	6 24	6 42	6s46	6 54	7 3	7e8	7s27	7 38	7 56
Catford Bridge	3 8	3s17	3e28	3s43	4 16		4 43	5 13	5s18	5 27	5e38	5 44	6 9	6e17	6s21	6 28	6 47	6s51	6 58	7 7	7e12	7s31	7 42	8 0
Lower Sydenham...	3 12	3s21	3e33	3s47	4 20		4 47	5 17	5s22		....	5 48	....	6e21	6s25	....	6 51	6s55	....		7e16	7s35	7 46	....
New Beckenham ...	3 15	3s24	3e36	3s50	4 23	4 25	4 50	5 20	5s25		5e43	5 51	6 14	6e24	6s28	6 33	6 54	6s58	7 3		7e19	7s38	7 49	8 5
Clock House......	3 18	3s28	3e40	3s54	4s26	4 28	4 53	5 23	5s28	Except Saturdays.	5e46	5 55	6 17	6e27	6s31	6 36	6 57	7s1	7 6	Except Saturdays.	7e22	7s41	7 52	Except Saturdays.
Elmer's End......	Sats. only.	3s31	3e43	3s57	4s29	4 31	4 56	5 26	5s31		5e49	5 58		6e30	6s34	....	7 1	7s4			7e25	7s45	7 56	
Elmer's End dep.		3s40	3e46	4s15	....	4 32	5 0	Except Sats.	5s43		5e51	....	Except Sats.	6e34	6s35	Except Sats.	Except Sats.	7s11	Except Sats.		7e28	8s5	Except Sats.	
Eden Park		3s44	3e50	....	....	4 36	5 4		5s47		5e55	....		6e37	6s39			7s15			7e32	....		
West Wickham.		3s47	3e53	4s22	....	4 39	5 7		5s50		5e58	....		6e40	6s42			7s18			7e35	8s11		
Hayes...... arr.		3s51	3e57	4s26	....	4 43	5 11		5s54		6e2	....		6e44	6s46			7s22			7e39	8s15		
Woodside ‡ (below)	3 23	3s35	3e47	4s1	4s33	4 36	5 0	5 30	5s35	5 38	5e53	6 2	6 22	6e34	6s39	6 41	7 4	7s8	7 11		7e29	7s49	8 0	
Croydon * .... arr.	3 26	3s38	3e50	4s4	4s36	4 39	5 3	5 33	5s38	5 42	5e56	6 5	6 25	6e37	6s42	6 44	7 7	7s11	7 14		7e32	7s52	8 3	
Beckenham Jn. "	....	3s32	3e44	3s57	4 29	....	4 55	5 27	5s31	....	5e52	5 58	6 20	6s30	6s34	6 42	7 1	7s5	....		7e25	7s44	7 55	8 10

Week Days—*Continued.* / **Sundays.**

Down.	aft	aft	aft	aft	aft	aft	aft	aft	aft	ngt.	mrn	mrn	mrn	aft	aft	aft	aft	aft	aft	aft	aft	aft	aft	aft	aft	aft
Charing Cross..dep.	7 40	8 13	d	9 5	9 26	9 58	1045	1112	1133	1218	740	9 8	1117	1235	138	...	238	3 38	438	538	638	738	838	9 38	1038	1122
Waterloo Junction.	7 42	8 15	....	9 7	9 28	10 0	....	1114	....	....	742	910	1119	1237	140	...	240	3 40	440	540	640	740	840	9 40	....	1124
Cannon Street.....	7 49	8 23	8 48	9 14	9 35	10 8	....	....	....	....	751	...	....	1244	...	...	...	....	...	...	...	...	...	....	....	....
London Bridge.....	7 52	8 26	8 51	9 17	9 39	1011	1051	1119	....	1224	754	915	1124	1247	145	...	245	3 45	445	545	645	745	846	9 45	1044	1129
New Cross..........	....	8 34	8 58	9 24	....	1019	....	1126	....	....	8 2	922	1132	1254	152	...	252	3 52	452	552	652	752	854	9 52	....	1136
St. John's	....	8 37	9 1	9 27	....	1022	....	1129	....	....	8 5	925	1135	1257	155	...	255	3 55	455	555	655	755	857	9 55	....	1139
Lewisham Junction	8s2	8 40	9 4	9 30	9 49	1025	11 0	1132	....	1234	8 8	928	1138	1259	157	...	258	3 58	458	558	658	758	9 0	9 58	1053	1142
Lady Well..........	8 3	8 43	9 7	9 33	9 52	1028	11 3	1135	1147	1237	811	931	1141	1 2	2 0	...	3 1	4 1	5 1	6 1	7 1	8 1	9 3	10 1	1056	1145
Catford Bridge.....	8 7	8 47	9 11	9 37	9 56	1032	11 6	1139	1151	1241	814	934	1144	1 5	2 3	...	3 4	4 4	5 4	6 4	7 4	8 4	9 6	10 4	1059	1148
Lower Sydenham...	8 11	8 51	9 15	9 41	....	1036	....	1143	....	1245	818	938	1148	1 9	2 7	...	3 8	4 8	5 8	6 8	7 8	8 8	910	10 8	....	1152
New Beckenham ...	8 14	8 54	9 18	9 44	....	1039	....	1146	1156	1248	821	941	1151	1 12	210	...	311	4 11	511	611	711	811	913	1011	....	1155
Clock House......	8 18	8 57	9 24	9 48	....	1042	1112	....	12 0	1251	824	944	1154	1 15	213	...	314	4 14	514	614	714	814	917	1014	11 5	1158
Elmer's End......	8 21	9 0	9 27	9 51	....	1045	....	....	12 3	1254	827	947	1157	1 18	216	...	318	4 18	518	618	718	818	920	1018	11 8	12 2
Elmer's End dep.	....	9 2	Except Sats.	9 54	....	1048	....	a	12 6	....	832	950	12 0	1 19	218	250	335	....	...	620	...	819	...	1021	....	....
Eden Park......	....	....		....	....	....	....	....	....	....	...	953	....	1 22	221	...	338	....	...	...	...	...	...	....	....	....
West Wickham.	....	9 8		10 0	....	1054	....	a	1212	....	837	956	12 5	1 25	224	255	341	....	...	625	...	824	...	1026	....	....
Hayes...... arr.	....	9 12		10 4	....	1058	....	a	1216	....	841	100	1210	1 29	228	259	345	....	...	629	...	828	...	1030	....	....
Woodside ‡ (below)	8 25	9 4	9 31	9 55	10 4	1049	1117	....	12 7	1258	831	951	12 1	1 22	220	...	322	4 22	522	622	722	822	925	1022	1112	12 6
Croydon * .... arr.	8 28	9 7	9 34	9 58	....	1052	1120	....	1210	1 1	834	954	12 4	1 25	223	...	325	4 25	525	625	725	825	928	1025	1115	12 9
Beckenham Jn. arr.	8 22	9 0	9 22	9 50	....	1045	....	1150	12 2	1251	827	947	1157	1 18	215	...	317	4 17	517	617	717	817	920	1017	....	12 1

a Wednesday nights only.

d Runs to Orpington.

e Except Saturdays.

s Saturdays only.

* Addiscombe Road.

‡ Woodside and South Norwood.

The evening weekday down service from 13th September
1958, the first to show a basic 20-minute interval service.

LONDON, NEW BECKENHAM, HAYES, ADDISCOMBE and SANDERSTEAD

2—All Trains on this page are Second class only

Down — Mondays to Fridays—continued (pm)

LONDON																									
„ Charing Cross. dep	..	5 18	5 21	..	..	5 49	5 51	..	..	6 46	12	6 19	..	6 25	..	6 39	..	6 46	..	..	7 0	..	7 10
„ Waterloo	..	5 20	5 23	..	..	5 51	5 53	..	..	6 7	6 14	6 21	..	6 27	..	6 41	..	6 49	..	..	7 2	..	7 12
„ Cannon Street	5 20	..	..	5 34	5 41	..	6 6	..	..	..	..	..	..	..	6 33	..	..	..	6 55	..	..	..
London Bridge	5 23	5 25	5 28	5 37	5 44	5 55	5 58	6 9	..	6 11	6 18	6 26	..	6 31	6 36	6 45	..	6 53	..	6 58	7 6	..	7 17
New Cross	5 29	5 32	..	5 43	..	..	6 4	..	..	6 18	6 25	..	..	6 37	6 42	6 51	..	6 58	..	7 5	7 12	..	..
St. John's	..	..	5 38	..	..	..	..	..	..	6 20	..	..	..	..	..	..	..	..	..	7 14	..	7 24
Lewisham	5 32	..	5 40	5 46	..	6 8	..	..	6 28	..	..	6 40	..	6 54	..	..	..	7 8	7 16	..	..
Lady Well	..	5 37	5 43	5 48	5 55	..	6 10	..	6 24	6 30	..	6 42	6 46	6 56	..	7 3	..	7 10	7 18	..	7 27
Catford Bridge	5 35	5 39	5 45	5 51	5 57	6 6	12	6 20	..	6 26	6 33	6 38	..	6 45	6 49	6 58	..	7 5	..	7 13	7 21	..	7 30
Lower Sydenham	5 38	5 42	5 48	5 54	..	6 0	9	6 15	6 23	..	6 29	6 36	..	6 48	6 52	7 1	..	7 8	..	7 16	7 24	..	7 33
New Beckenham	..	5 44	5 50	5 56	..	2	6 11	6 17	6 25	..	6 31	6 38	6 42	..	6 50	6 54	7 3	..	7 10	..	7 20	7 26	..	7 35
Clock House	5 41	5 47	5 53	5 58	..	5	6 14	6 20	6 27	..	6 34	6 40	6 44	..	6 52	6 56	7 6	..	7 13	..	..	7 28	..	7 37
Elmer's End { arr	5 43	5 49	5 55	6 0	..	7	6 16	6 22	6 29	..	6 36	6 42	6 46	..	6 54	6 58	7 8	..	7 15	..	..	7 30	..	7 39
Elmer's End { dep	5 43	5 49	5 55	6 0	..	7	6 16	6 23	6 29	6 33	6 36	6 42	6 46	6 50	6 54	6 58	7 8	7 11	7 15	7 21	..	7 30	7 36	7 39

Eden Park dep	..	5 53	..	6 4	..	6 19	..	6 33	..	6 39	..	6 50	..	..	7 2	..	..	7 18	..	..	7 34	..	7 43
West Wickham	..	5 55	..	6 7	..	6 22	..	6 35	..	6 42	..	6 52	..	..	7 4	..	..	7 21	..	..	7 36	..	7 45
Hayes arr	..	5 59	..	6 10	..	6 25	..	6 39	..	6 45	..	6 56	..	..	7 8	..	..	7 24	..	..	7 40	..	7 49

Woodside	5 46	..	5 57	..	6 10	..	6 26	..	6 35	..	6 45	..	6 52	6 57	..	7 10	7 13	..	7 23	..	..	7 38	..
Addiscombe arr	..	6 0	..	..	6 29	..	6 38	..	..	6 55	7 0	..	7 14	..	..	7 26	..	..	..	..

Bingham Road	5 48	..	..	6 12	..	..	..	6 48	..	..	..	7 15	..	..	..	7 40	..
Coombe Road	..	..	..	6 15	..	..	..	6 51	..	..	..	7 18	..	..	..	7 43	..
Selsdon	5 51	..	..	6 18	..	..	..	6 55	..	..	..	7 20	..	..	..	7 45	..
Sanderstead arr	5 54	..	..	6 20	..	..	..	6 57	..	..	..	7 23	..	..	..	7 48	..

Down — Mondays to Fridays—continued (pm)

LONDON												
„ Charing Cross. dep	7 15	..	..	7 30	..	..	7 51	..	..	8 11	..	..	8 31	..	..	8 51	..	..	9 11	..
„ Waterloo	7 17	..	..	7 32	..	..	7 53	..	..	8 13	..	..	8 33	..	..	8 53	..	..	9 13	..
„ Cannon Street	..	..	..	..	..	7 47	..	..	..	..	..	..	..	..	..	..	..	..
London Bridge	7 22	..	..	7 38	..	7 50	7 58	..	..	8 18	..	..	8 38	..	..	8 58	..	..	9 18	..
New Cross	7 27	..	..	7 43	..	7 56	8 3	..	..	8 23	..	..	8 43	..	..	9 3	..	..	9 23	..
St. John's	..	..	..	7 46	..	7 58	8 6	..	..	8 26	..	..	8 46	..	..	9 6	..	..	9 26	..
Lewisham	..	..	..	7 48	..	8 0	8 8	..	..	8 28	..	..	8 48	..	..	9 8	..	..	9 28	..
Lady Well	7 32	..	..	7 50	..	8 2	8 10	..	..	8 30	..	..	8 50	..	..	9 10	..	..	9 30	..
Catford Bridge	7 34	..	..	7 52	..	8 5	8 12	..	..	8 32	..	..	8 52	..	..	9 12	..	..	9 32	..
Lower Sydenham	7 37	..	..	7 55	..	8 8	8 15	..	..	8 35	..	..	8 55	..	..	9 15	..	..	9 35	..
New Beckenham	7 39	..	..	7 57	..	8 10	8 17	..	..	8 37	..	..	8 57	..	..	9 17	..	..	9 37	..
Clock House	7 42	..	..	8 0	..	..	8 20	..	..	8 40	..	..	9 0	..	..	9 20	..	..	9 40	..
Elmer's End { arr	7 44	..	..	8 2	..	..	8 22	..	..	8 42	..	..	9 2	..	..	9 22	..	..	9 42	..
Elmer's End { dep	7 44	7 48	..	8 2	8 6	..	8 22	..	8 26	..	8 42	..	8 46	..	9 2	9 6	..	9 22	9 26	..	9 42	9 46

Eden Park dep	..	..	..	8 5	..	..	8 25	..	..	8 45	..	..	9 5	..	..	9 25	..	..	9 45	..
West Wickham	..	..	..	8 8	..	..	8 28	..	..	8 48	..	..	9 8	..	..	9 28	..	..	9 48	..
Hayes arr	..	..	..	8 11	..	..	8 31	..	..	8 51	..	..	9 11	..	..	9 31	..	..	9 51	..

Woodside	7 46	7 50	..	..	8 8	..	..	8 28	..	..	8 48	..	..	9 8	..	..	9 28	..	..	9 48
Addiscombe arr	7 49	7 53	..	..	..	..	8 31	..	..	..	..	..	..	..	9 31	..	..	..

Bingham Road	..	..	..	8 10	..	..	..	..	..	8 50	..	..	9 10	..	..	..	9 50
Coombe Road	..	..	..	8 13	..	..	..	..	..	8 53	..	..	9 13	..	..	..	9 53
Selsdon	..	..	..	8 15	..	..	..	..	..	8 55	..	..	9 15	..	..	..	9 55
Sanderstead arr	..	..	..	8 18	..	..	..	..	..	8 58	..	..	9 18	..	..	..	9 58

Down — Mondays to Fridays—continued (pm)

LONDON											night	night
„ Charing Cross. dep	9 31	..	..	9 51	..	..	1011	..	..	1031	..	..	11 1	..	..	1144	..	..	..
„ Waterloo	9 33	..	..	9 53	..	..	1013	..	..	1033	..	..	11 3	..	..	1146	..	..	..
„ Cannon Street	..	..	..	..	..	..	..	..	..	..	..	..	..	..	..	..	..	..
London Bridge	9 38	..	..	9 58	..	..	1018	..	..	1038	..	..	11 8	..	..	1151	..	..	..
New Cross	9 43	..	..	10 3	..	..	1023	..	..	1043	..	..	1113	..	..	1156	..	..	..
St. John's	9 46	..	..	10 6	..	..	1026	..	..	1046	..	..	1116	..	..	1159	..	..	..
Lewisham	9 48	..	..	10 8	..	..	1028	..	..	1048	..	..	1118	..	..	12 1	..	..	..
Lady Well	9 50	..	..	1010	..	..	1030	..	..	1050	..	..	1120	..	..	12 3	..	..	..
Catford Bridge	9 52	..	..	1012	..	..	1032	..	..	1052	..	..	1122	..	..	12 5	..	..	..
Lower Sydenham	9 55	..	..	1015	..	..	1035	..	..	1055	..	..	1125	..	..	12 8	..	..	..
New Beckenham	9 57	..	..	1017	..	..	1037	..	..	1057	..	..	1127	..	..	1210	..	..	..
Clock House	10 0	..	..	1020	..	..	1040	..	..	11 0	..	..	1130	..	..	1213	..	..	..
Elmer's End { arr	10 2	..	..	1022	..	..	1042	..	..	11 2	..	..	1132	..	..	1215	..	..	..
Elmer's End { dep	10 2	10 6	..	1022	..	1026	..	1042	..	1046	11 2	11 6	..	1132	1136	..	1215	..	1218	..	1239

Eden Park dep	10 5	..	..	1025	..	..	1045	..	..	11 5	..	..	1135	..	..	1218	..	..	..
West Wickham	10 8	..	..	1028	..	..	1048	..	..	11 8	..	..	1138	..	..	1221	..	..	..
Hayes arr	1011	..	..	1031	..	..	1051	..	..	1111	..	..	1141	..	..	1224	..	..	..

Woodside	..	10 8	..	..	1028	..	..	1048	..	..	11 8	..	..	1138	..	..	1220	..	1241
Addiscombe arr	..	..	..	1031	..	..	1051	..	..	1111	..	..	1141	..	..	1223	..	1244

Bingham Road	..	1010	..	..	..	..	..	..	..	..	..	..	..	..	..	..
Coombe Road	..	1013	..	..	..	..	..	..	..	..	..	..	..	..	..	..
Selsdon	..	1015	..	..	..	..	..	..	..	..	..	..	..	..	..	..
Sanderstead arr	..	1018	..	..	..	..	..	..	..	..	..	..	..	..	..	..

LONDON BRIDGE

1. From left to right are terminal buildings of the former SER and LBSCR, flanked by the Terminus Hotel. They are seen in the 1930s, not long before being severely bombed by Nazi aircraft. (Lens of Sutton)

2. An aerial view in the early 1950s includes Cannon Street station (top right) and part of the triangular junction on the Charing Cross line (top left). The first station on the site was the terminus of the London & Greenwich Railway (1836). Next came the London and Croydon Railway (1839), whose terminus was built to the north of the L&G's. They exchanged stations in 1844 to obviate conflicting movements. The SER's through lines (right) were opened in 1864 and the LBSCR added six platforms on the south side of the station (left) in 1850. The low level SER platforms (centre) were roofed over until 1907 and were used as the Continental Goods Depot between 1864 and 1901. (British Rail)

The expansion of and the subsequent alterations to the station were very complex and can be more fully understood by reference to the companion albums - *London Bridge to East Croydon, Charing Cross to Dartford* and *Charing Cross to Orpington.*

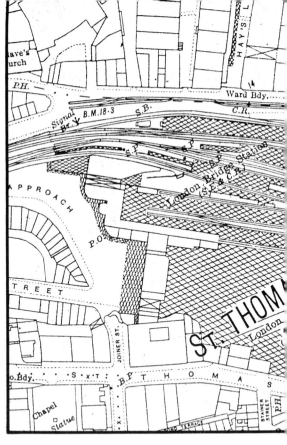

The 1916 map indicates the relationship of the SECR and LBSCR stations.

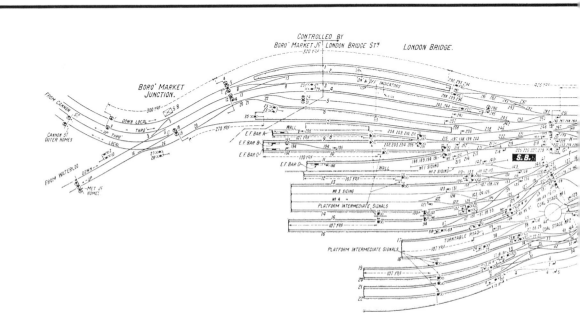

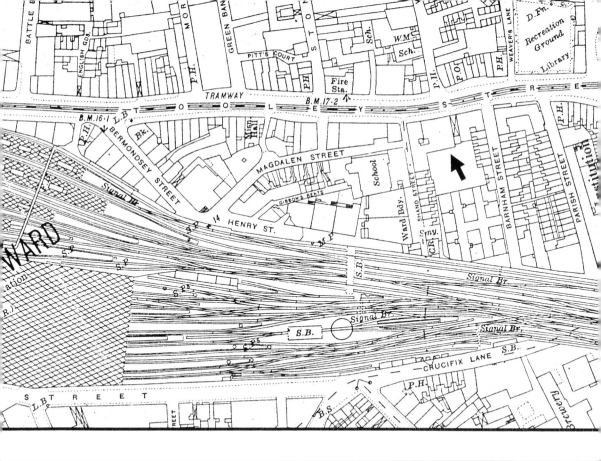

On 17th June 1928 the platforms were re-numbered, as shown on this 1930 diagram of the station's first colour light signalling installation. It replaced four mechanical signal boxes within the station area, these having a total of 574 levers. E.F.Bar refers to "electric fouling bar", an elongated treadle which detected isolated locomotives or vehicles standing near buffers and revealed their presence on the illuminated diagram in the signal box.

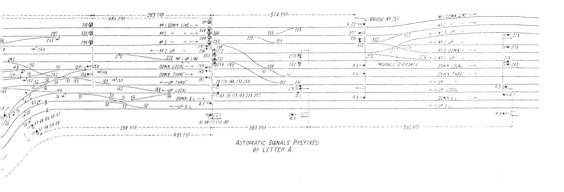

AUTOMATIC SIGNALS PREFIXED
BY LETTER A.

3. The two footbridges to the high level platforms are seen above the first and third coaches of the 5.20pm to Tunbridge Wells West on 22nd April 1948. Q class no. 534 is at platform 9, the only one to retain an engine release crossover at that time. (J.H.Aston)

4. Class I3 no. 32021 approaches the platforms seen in the previous picture and passes the massive water tank. The train is the 7.47am from Tunbridge Wells West on 13th July 1950. (J.H.Aston)

5. Platform 6 is viewed from platform 4 on 3rd December 1952. There was no platform 5 although the number was used to refer to the through up goods line of which only a stump then remained. It had been used to hold transfer freights waiting to use the Snow Hill line, now designated "Thameslink". Such transfers were prohibited during peak hours. (D.Cullum)

6. Platforms 1, 2 and 3 were for down trains from both Charing Cross and Cannon Street and all had these indicators. In 1976 the three platforms were dedicated to Cannon Street trains; 1 down, 2 reversible and 3 up. (British Rail)

7. Outside the peak hours the low level platforms were used for mail and parcel traffic, as is evident in May 1953, as class E1 no. 31165 leaves with the "Midday Vans". The heap of ash (left) had been left by engines standing in the short no.1 siding, only the catch point of which is visible. (P.Hay)

8. Platform 11 (left) was too short for passenger trains and often contained vans at peak times. The same locomotive is seen on 1st April 1954, while another short van train stands at platform 10, probably awaiting mailbags. (H.C.Casserley)

9. The south-west corner of the station, along with the Terminus Hotel, was almost completely destroyed by enemy action in December 1940. Over 30 years were to elapse before rebuilding was complete.
(British Rail)

10. Owing to the loss of so many of the railway buildings, a temporary booking office was erected on the concourse, opposite the barriers of platforms 13 and 14. The main roof of the station lost all its glass during the war.
(British Rail)

11. Another view from the 1950s shows the uncomfortable mix of morning rush-hour passengers, parcel traffic and Royal Mail vans. On the left is platform 16, the longest at the station, and on the right is the gap created by the Luftwaffe. (British Rail)

12. On the left is the northern wall of the former LBSCR train shed. A hole was cut in it in 1928 to give access to the former SECR platforms and a ticket barrier installed beyond the left border of this picture. Platform renumbering in 1976 resulted in no. 13 becoming no. 10. (British Rail)

13. The "Brighton" side of the station was lofty and spacious when compared with the cramped and awkward "Chatham" platforms. BR class 4 2-6-4T no. 80018 accelerates the 12.47pm along platform 16 towards Tunbridge Wells West on 4th April 1959. Platforms 20-22 were later closed, their site being used for railway offices and a new panel box which came into use on 20th July 1975. (J.H.Aston)

14. When opened in 1928 the signal box levers controlled 216 signal functions and 79 points, two illuminated diagrams being provided. The "Brighton Belle" was an unusual visitor on 19th April 1969, having been diverted from Victoria due to engineering works. (J.Scrace)

15. A flashback to 1928 shows the manufacture of the interlocking frame for the 311 levers provided in the new signal box. The signal current was 110 volt AC while the points were operated by 130volt DC from accumulators charged by motor generators powered by the 650 volt DC traction current.
(Railway Engineer)

3rd · SINGLE   SINGLE · 3rd

0142

Ladywell to
Ladywell   Ladywell
Cannon St. or W'loo   Cannon St. or W'loo
CANNON STREET or WATERLOO

(S) 11d. H   FARE   11d. H (S)
For conditions see over For conditions see over

0142

16. As shown in some of the previous pictures, there were two bridges over the former SECR platforms, but only one was fully enclosed. It contained an indicator for up trains only. Both bridges were removed in the major rebuilding of 1973-77, the single replacement being a dreary windowless structure. (E.Wilmshurst)

17. The new footbridge penetrated the former boundary wall and spanned the terminal platforms, as seen on 31st March 1991 during a Gala Weekend. On show is Sandite unit no.008 and no.33047 with a snow plough. By then only one of the four low level platforms remained in use and was then numbered 8. Further major track alterations took place between 24th July and 16th August 1993 when the Charing Cross lines were closed to allow the slewing of platforms 4 to 6. (P.G.Barnes)

SPA ROAD

18. One mile from London Bridge was the temporary terminus of the London & Greenwich Railway (from 8th February until 14th December 1836). It closed in 1838 but a new station was opened in 1842. It was rebuilt on a new site in 1867 and closed finally on 15th March 1915. Two of the four platforms of the final station are seen in 1926. (H.C.Casserley)

Location maps and other pictures of **Spa Road appear in** *Charing Cross to Dartford (no.39)* **and** *Charing Cross to Orpington (nos.38 and 39).*

19. The entrance is seen in 1957. Few Mid-Kent trains called here or at the other short lived stations to the east; Commercial Road (1856-66) and Southwark Park (1902-15). These were in similar elevated positions, most of the route to Greenwich having been built on brick arches. (A.E.Bennett)

NEW CROSS

The 1893 map reveals that two of the through lines each had two platform faces. The turntable was for the use of Metropolitan Railway engines.

20. North Kent East Junction is the point of divergence of the Greenwich and Lewisham lines and is east of the Corbetts Lane Junction where the Croydon line turns south. This box is at the former junction and was in use from 1st December 1929 until 16th April 1976. Behind the miniature levers are signal repeaters and above them are rotary train describers for each route. This was the first box to have electrical interlocking. (Railway Engineer)

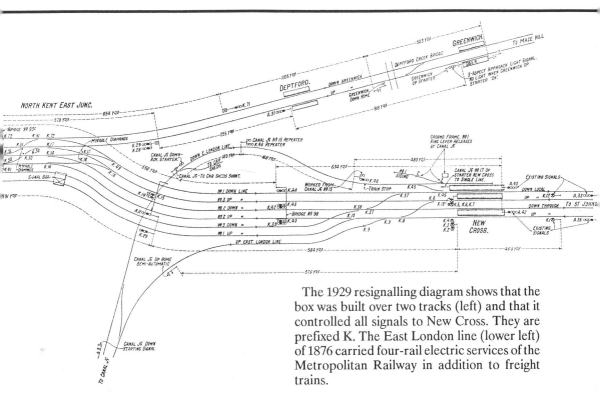

The 1929 resignalling diagram shows that the box was built over two tracks (left) and that it controlled all signals to New Cross. They are prefixed K. The East London line (lower left) of 1876 carried four-rail electric services of the Metropolitan Railway in addition to freight trains.

21. New Cross up signals are seen in transition in 1929, with New Cross "A" Box in the distance and soon to close (1st December 1929). Centre is a Metropolitan train on the East London line. Note that the up local signals have a route indicator. The installation of cluster signals soon ceased. (Railway Engineer)

22. The connection between the East London line from Whitechapel and the local line from London Bridge is seen from a down train. The station was "New Cross (SER)" from 1854 until 1923 when "New Cross (LBSCR)" became "New Cross Gate". (A.E.Bennett)

23. The London Transport line is on the right as class E1 no. 31165 is seen for the third time in this volume. It is speeding south on the main line with a hop pickers special to Paddock Wood on 2nd September 1958, the leading vans containing prams and handcarts loaded with bedding and food. (J.Scrace)

24. In 1975 this building was erected in Amersham Vale and its predecessor on the New Cross Road bridge was demolished to allow the bridge to be rebuilt. The platforms were lengthened under it in 1993. They are lettered A to D instead of being numbered and there has been no platform on the up fast line since the 1975 rebuilding. (J.Scrace)

ST. JOHNS

St. Johns Church and St. Johns Road are in the centre of this c1870 map (at 6" to 1 mile) but the station is not marked as it did not open until 1st June 1873. It was sited near the **S** of **SOUTH EASTERN RAILWAY**. Near the **H** is the bridge of the LCDR line from Nunhead to Blackheath Hill shown under construction. It opened on 18th September 1871; was extended to Greenwich Park on 1st October 1888 and is described in our *Holborn Viaduct to Lewisham* album. Lewisham station is on the right and on the right border is the line to Blackheath and Woolwich. Long gone are the brickfields, limekiln, pottery, silk mill, Anchor Brewery and engine works in Blackheath Road.

25. In the distance is the portal of the 87yd long Tanners Hill Tunnel beyond which is New Cross station. The station was opened to serve the developing residential district, the original buildings remaining in use until replaced in August 1983. (J.Scrace)

26. The 7.24am London Bridge to Ramsgate service was headed by class D1 no.31739 on 3rd June 1961. On the left is the loading gauge over the track leading to the sidings, which were mainly used for storage. Until 1926 there had been five platforms, the southernmost being a bay. (J.Scrace)

27. The island platform between the main lines was removed in 1973, allowing the straightening of the up main (centre). The line on the right was opened on 29th March 1976 and was signalled for bidirectional working. The arch on the left of the previous picture was eliminated and replaced by a high level concrete span to accommodate the raised track which was laid on a 1 in 45 gradient. The train on the left is proceeding towards Lewisham which is visible in the distance. (P.Davis)

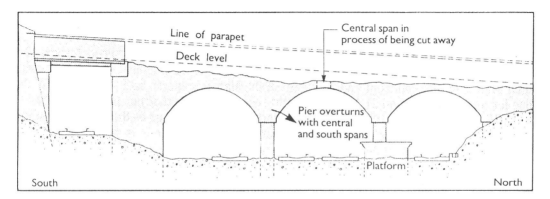

Line of parapet

Deck level

Central span in
process of being cut away

Pier overturns
with central
and south spans

Platform

South

North

The Lewisham disaster of 4th December 1957 is described in *Charing Cross to Orpington* and *Holborn Viaduct to Lewisham* and not repeated here. A less well known accident occurred on 13th June 1992 during the demolition of the bridge shown in picture 26. The diagram shows the situation at 10.30am. Two workmen died and several were injured. A new single span allowed the platforms to be lengthened.

28. The signal box was situated to the left of the train seen in the previous picture and was in use from 30th June 1929 until 8th December 1976. It was photographed in the previous year. (J.Scrace)

The 1893 edition of the 6" to 1 mile map has Blackheath Hill LCDR station top left, the sidings of St. Johns station on the left margin, those of Blackheath station on the right margin, Hither Green lower right and our route to Ladywell lower left.

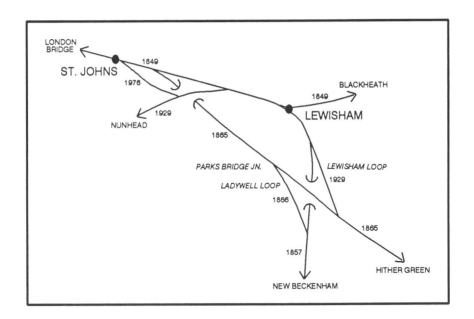

29. Approaching platform 1 is the 12.20pm Ramsgate to Victoria on 30th May 1959. This was an unusual sight, the train having been diverted from its usual route to run via Hither Green and Nunhead. The 1929 freight lines thus had additional value, as well as being used for local passenger trains. (J.J.Smith)

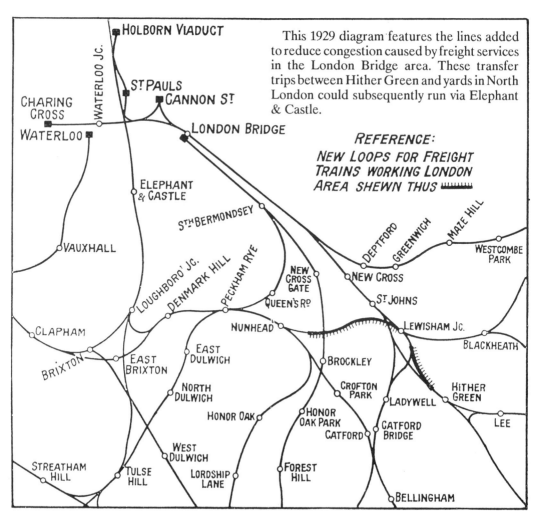

HOLBORN VIADUCT

This 1929 diagram features the lines added to reduce congestion caused by freight services in the London Bridge area. These transfer trips between Hither Green and yards in North London could subsequently run via Elephant & Castle.

WATERLOO JC.

St PAULS

CANNON St

CHARING CROSS

WATERLOO

LONDON BRIDGE

REFERENCE:
NEW LOOPS FOR FREIGHT
TRAINS WORKING LONDON
AREA SHEWN THUS ⊥⊥⊥⊥⊥

ELEPHANT & CASTLE

Sth BERMONDSEY

VAUXHALL

DEPTFORD

GREENWICH

MAZE HILL

WESTCOMBE PARK

LOUGHBORO' JC.

DENMARK HILL

PECKHAM RYE

NEW CROSS GATE

NEW CROSS

QUEEN'S Rd

St JOHNS

CLAPHAM

NUNHEAD

LEWISHAM JC.

BLACKHEATH

BRIXTON

EAST BRIXTON

EAST DULWICH

BROCKLEY

CROFTON PARK

LADYWELL

HITHER GREEN

NORTH DULWICH

HONOR OAK

HONOR OAK PARK

CATFORD

CATFORD BRIDGE

LEE

WEST DULWICH

STREATHAM HILL

TULSE HILL

LORDSHIP LANE

FOREST HILL

BELLINGHAM

30. Nos. 33203 and 33209 run towards Lewisham with empty aggregate wagons destined for Cliffe Brett Marine (see our *Branch Line to Allhallows*) on 23rd October 1986. They had started at 10.00 from Salfords. This use of the flyover had not been anticipated in 1929. (C.Wilson)

31. A 4EPB unit hammers the diamond crossings on 15th July 1992 as it approaches platform 2 while working the 12.23 Charing Cross to Hayes service. The 1929 flyover is on the left and the Blackheath lines are on the right. (M.Turvey)

Other views and maps of Lewisham appear in *Lewisham to Dartford, Holborn Viaduct to Lewisham* **and** *Charing Cross to Orpington.*

32. By the time this photograph was taken on 24th June 1993, about half of the Hayes trains were worked by the new Networker class 465 units, such as this example. No. 465009 is working the 17.28 from Cannon Street. (B.Morrison)

33. We return now to look at the main line. Speeding south under the viaduct on 23rd October 1975 is unit no. 7855 forming part of the 13.10 Charing Cross to Margate service. Passing over the supports erected hastily after the 1957 disaster is a class 33 diesel working the 12.25 cement train from Northfleet to Toton. (J.Scrace)

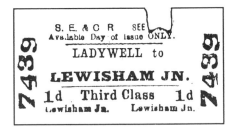

34. Photographed on the same day, Parks Bridge Junction box was situated north of the junction of the Ladywell Loop with the main line. It opened on the same day as St. Johns Box but closed on 8th February 1976. (J.Scrace)

35. A panorama on 3rd September 1992 includes the 09.18 Hayes to Charing Cross passing under the main line approaching Lewisham. In the foreground is the 1929 Lewisham Loop - the Ladywell Loop is obscured by the embankment. (J.Scrace)

LADYWELL

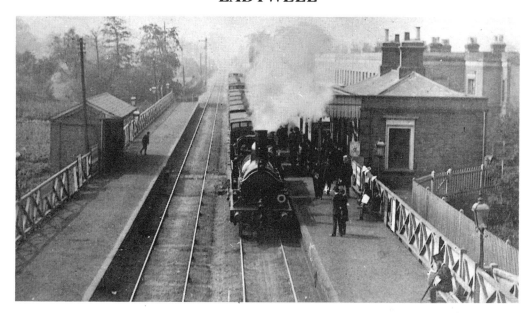

36. The station opened with the line on 1st January 1857 and gradually developed a business traffic to London. This undated photograph includes a top hatted gentleman awaiting an up train. (D.Cullum coll.)

The 1916 map shows a crossover but fails to mark the position of the signal box which was in use until 30th June 1929. The name originates from an ancient well situated close to the church of St. Mary the Virgin - "Our Lady".

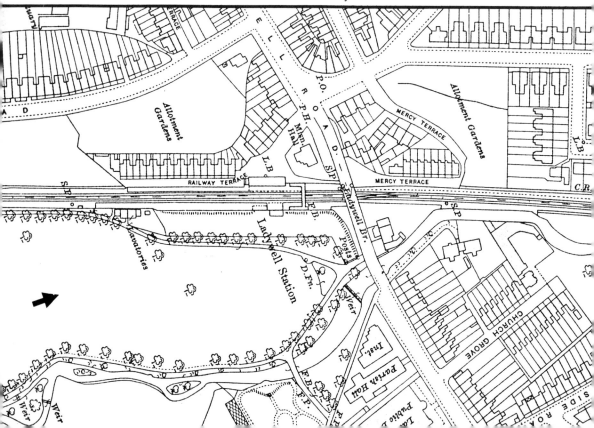

37. A northward view in 1955 shows the recent platform extensions to accommodate 10-car trains. The down side is awaiting new gas lights at a time when such equipment was very outdated. (British Rail)

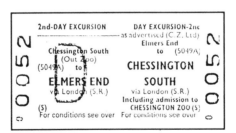

2nd-DAY EXCURSION	DAY EXCURSION-2nd
	as advertised (C.Z, Ltd)
	Elmers End
Chessington South	to (5049A)
(Out Zoo)	
(5049A) to	CHESSINGTON
ELMERS END	SOUTH
via London (S.R.)	via London (S.R.)
	Including admission to
(S)	CHESSINGTON ZOO (S)
For conditions see over	For conditions see over

C 0052 C 0052

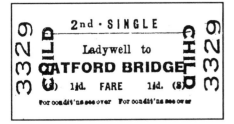

2nd · SINGLE

Ladywell to
CATFORD BRIDGE
(8) 1½d. FARE 1½d. (8)
For condit'ns see over For condit'ns see over

CHILD 3329 CHILD 3329

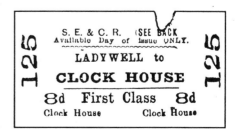

S. E. & C. R. (SEE BACK
Available Day of Issue ONLY.

LADYWELL to
CLOCK HOUSE
8d First Class 8d
Clock House Clock House

125 125

38.   Devoid of end warning panels, green painted 4EPB unit no. S5196 forms the 1.18pm Hayes to Charing Cross on 28th September 1958. The buildings at the far end of the down platform are the public lavatories of the recreation ground, now a nature reserve. (J.Scrace)

39.   A 1992 view reveals that the station retained most of its historic features, unlike others on the route. The reason for passengers having to stand in the rain to issue their own tickets is not apparent. Most of the stations on the route retained ticket offices in the morning peak hours. (J.Scrace)

CATFORD BRIDGE

40. The station opened with the line but did not have a goods yard until the 20th century. Beyond the top hatted gentleman (the station master?) is a crossover and a double armed signal post, probably then the only one at the station. (Lens of Sutton)

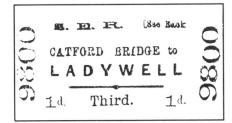

41. The road (and tram tracks) over the Ravensbourne River and the Mid-Kent line is on the right. This is Catford Bridge after which the station is named. On the left of this view is the commencement of Station Road - its continuation is seen on the left of the previous picture. (Lens of Sutton)

The 1916 edition has the Mid-Kent line of the former SER to the right of the former LCDR route from Nunhead to Shortlands. The latter is featured in our *Crystal Palace (H.L.) and Catford Loop* album. The tramway passing over Catford Bridge itself was in use from 29th May 1913 until 6th October 1951.

42. A closer view of the up side building includes the coal merchant's order office, a common feature of suburban stations. The gateway to the goods yard is evident, its main traffic being household coal. (Lens of Sutton)

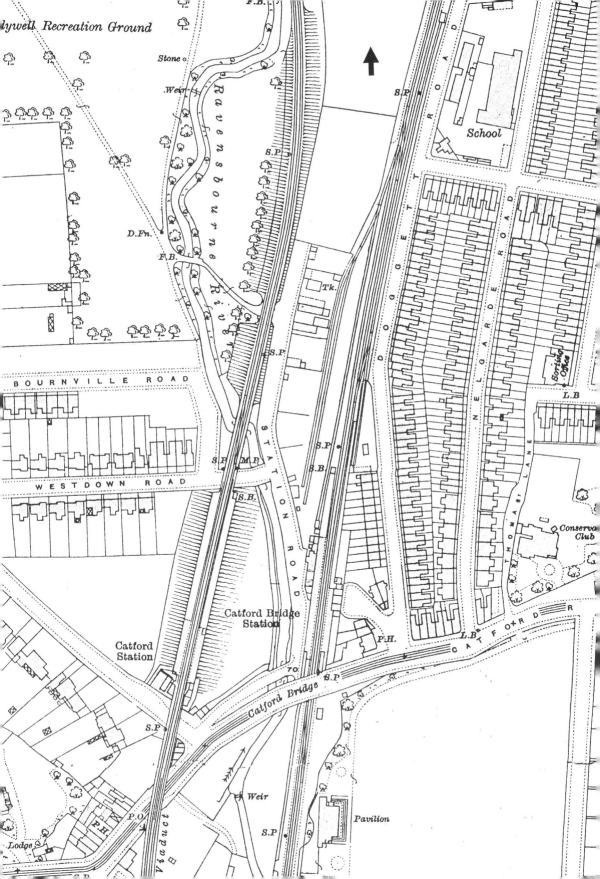

lywell Recreation Ground

Stone

Weir

Ravensbourne River

D.Fn.

F.B.

F.B.

S.P.

S.P.

Tk.

S.P.

ROAD

School

DOGGETT

S.P.

NELGARDE ROAD

Sorting Office

L.B

BOURNVILLE ROAD

WESTDOWN ROAD

S.P. M.P.

S.B.

S.P.

S.B.

STATION ROAD

S.T.THOMAS' LANE

Conserva Club

Catford Bridge
Station

Catford
Station

P.H.

L.B

CATFORD

S.P.

70

S.P.

Catford Bridge

Weir

P.H.

P.O.

Lodge

Viaduct

S.P.

Pavilion

S.P.

43. Snowfall at the end of December 1962 was a prelude to much more to come and the worst winter in living memory. Rail services were severely disrupted, water mains froze underground, coal froze together in wagons and ice remained for nearly three months. (J.Scrace)

44. A closer look at the signal box shown in the previous picture shows it to be of standard SER style with weather boards and sash windows. The box closed on 3rd April 1971. In the background of this 1969 picture is the Catford Loop line. Its bridge over the Mid-Kent was rebuilt in September 1928. (J.Scrace)

45. A 1970 southward view shows (right) cars parked on the site of the former goods yard which closed on 23rd March 1968 for general traffic, but remained in use for coal a little longer. On the left is the refuge siding marked on the map. (British Rail)

46. Having just passed Catford Greyhound Stadium which has generated much railway revenue, the 13.23 from Charing Cross to Hayes pulls into the down platform. The new footbridge is evident but out of view is a footbridge to the stadium. (J.Scrace)

LOWER SYDENHAM

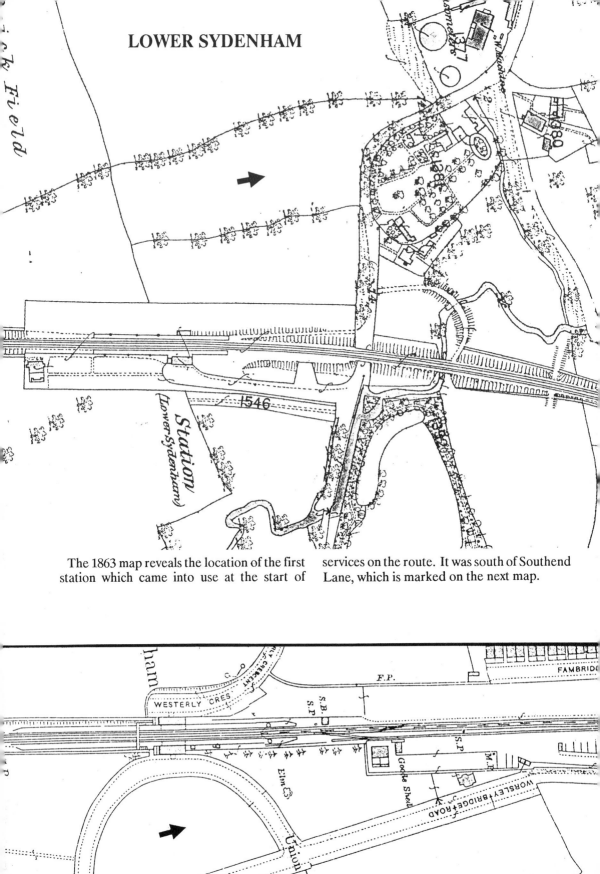

The 1863 map reveals the location of the first station which came into use at the start of services on the route. It was south of Southend Lane, which is marked on the next map.

```
 C        3rd-SINGLE  C
 H   1696                H   1696
 I   New Beckenham  to  I
 L                       L
 D   LOWER SYDENHAM  D
    (S) 1d.H  FARE 1d.H (S)
       For Conditions see over.
```

```
         S. E. & C. R  (SEE BACK)
         Available Day of Issue ONLY.
 0        Catford Bridge to       0
 8  (S.1)                         8
 0  LOWER SYDENHAM  0
 4  Revised Fare    Revised Fare  4
       2d.   Third Class   2d.
    Lower Sydenham      or Sydenham
```

The 1916 edition indicates the position of the station (left) since 1906. Marked nearby is the single goods siding. On the right page is the complex trackwork of the gasworks. The connection was made in 1878, coal being conveyed from Erith Wharf. The retort houses have tracks along each side.

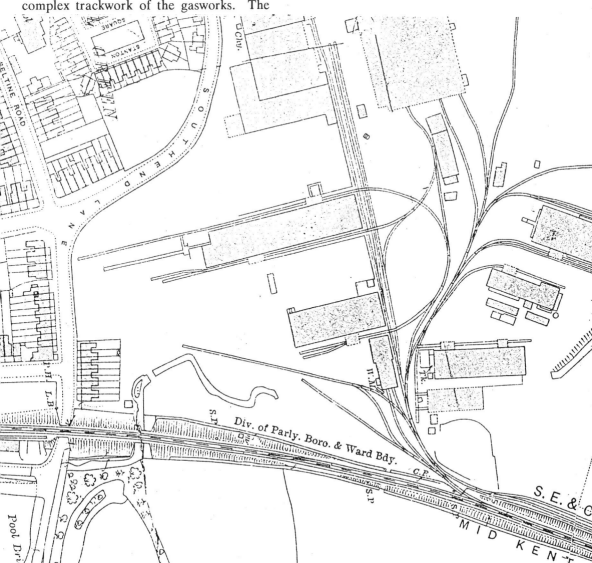

47. This is the down side of the second station, which opened in 1906. The SECR adopted the design that had been employed by the SER for many decades, timber framing and cladding being quite economical. (Lens of Sutton)

48. A northward view in 1961 includes the signal box, siding and goods shed in the distance. The first station had been beyond them. The station lighting is in transition from gas to electric. In the 1850s the LBSCR had a lineside gas main from its own gasworks at New Cross (Gate) to Sydenham station. (J.Scrace)

49. Owing to high charges demanded for use of the railway gas pipe, a local works was established in 1852. In 1854 this became the Crystal Palace District Gasworks and new premises were built south of Southend Lane. The site north of this road was developed later and became rail connected. Further expansion took place after 1904, when the name was changed to the South Suburban Gas Company. By 1914, 150,000 tons of coal and 250,000 gallons of oil was passing over the siding. The total traffic was about 300,000 tons in 1950, by which time the works was nationalised and controlled by the South Eastern Gas Board. It closed on 22nd April 1969 and 4½ miles of internal track became redundant. *Anne* and *Elizabeth* are seen near retort house no. 5 between the wars. (SEGAS)

Locomotives

5	Black, Hawthorn	1883	
8	Black, Hawthorn	1889	
16	Aveling & Porter	1899	(Geared)
20	Avonside	1909	*Mary*
21	Avonside	1914	*Anne*
	Avonside	1922	*Elizabeth*
	Planet diesel	1955	*Elizabeth II*

All had 0-4-0 wheel arrangements
Mary and *Anne* to Eastbourne Gasworks
Elizabeth to Croydon Gasworks 1955

50. The leading two-coach set of a 10-car train passes the disused goods shed on 6th June 1969, goods facilities having been withdrawn on 20th June 1966. The signal box remained in use until 3rd April 1971. Gas holder frames are on both sides of the picture. (J.Scrace)

51. The 12.23 Charing Cross to Hayes passes between the new buildings on 3rd September 1992, while the platforms are being lengthened in the background in readiness for the Networker class 465 trains which were introduced in the following year. (J.Scrace)

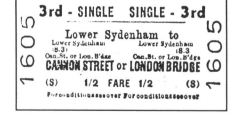

52. The chalet style of architecture was a great improvement upon the box-like CLASP buildings of the previous era of construction. One of the station's two footbridges is visible. (J.Scrace)

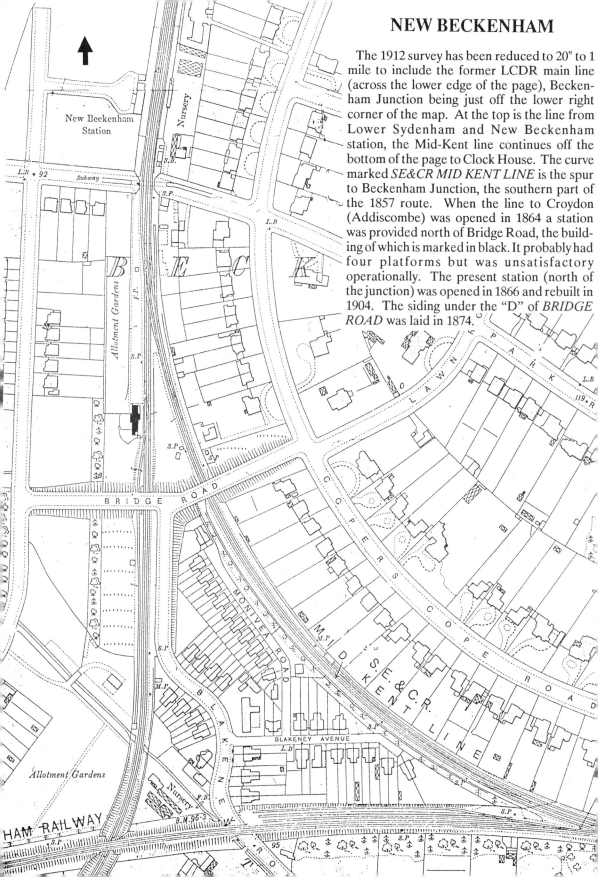

NEW BECKENHAM

The 1912 survey has been reduced to 20" to 1 mile to include the former LCDR main line (across the lower edge of the page), Beckenham Junction being just off the lower right corner of the map. At the top is the line from Lower Sydenham and New Beckenham station, the Mid-Kent line continues off the bottom of the page to Clock House. The curve marked *SE&CR MID KENT LINE* is the spur to Beckenham Junction, the southern part of the 1857 route. When the line to Croydon (Addiscombe) was opened in 1864 a station was provided north of Bridge Road, the building of which is marked in black. It probably had four platforms but was unsatisfactory operationally. The present station (north of the junction) was opened in 1866 and rebuilt in 1904. The siding under the "D" of *BRIDGE ROAD* was laid in 1874.

53. Down trains, such as this indistinct one, would often be divided here, a short front portion being taken on to Beckenham Junction. In the reverse direction this would be propelled round the spur and joined onto the rear of a waiting up train. This was the case until 1904 when the station was rebuilt with a centre road. (Lens of Sutton)

54. The centre road was useful for holding the branch engine between shunting movements or for use as a refuge for goods trains. This early 1920s view from the down platform shows the position of the subway.
(H.J.Patterson-Rutherford)

55. No. A360 is a Q class 0-4-4T from 1891 and is seen on the centre road on 27th February 1926, the day before electric services commenced. Withdrawn from service that year, the locomotive had been built for the SER. The middle road was eliminated in 1929, the joining and dividing of trains here having ceased in 1916. (H.C.Casserley)

56. A broad view of the signal box in 1969 includes the 15.35 from Charing Cross on 4th June. The station was rebuilt in 1904 and at about this time a pedestrian subway (foreground) replaced a level crossing here and the bridge south of the junction was built. (J.Scrace)

57. Looking north from Bridge Road in 1961 we see the buildings of the first station on the left, the line to Beckenham Junction on the right and the 1874 berthing siding in the left foreground. (J.Scrace)

58. A 1992 picture shows the new booking office. The platform canopies were reduced in length and the signal box was abolished on 27th September 1975. Part of the spur to Beckenham Junction was reduced to single line in 1987. (J.Scrace)

CLOCK HOUSE

59. The station opened in June 1890 and was to be called "Penge Road". A change of plan resulted in it being named after a nearby mansion, which was demolished about seven years later. This is a postcard view of the down platform. (Lens of Sutton)

The 1933 map shows the relationship of Chaffinch Brook to the railway. South of Clock House a trailing siding from the up line served the council depot and is shown on the next map.

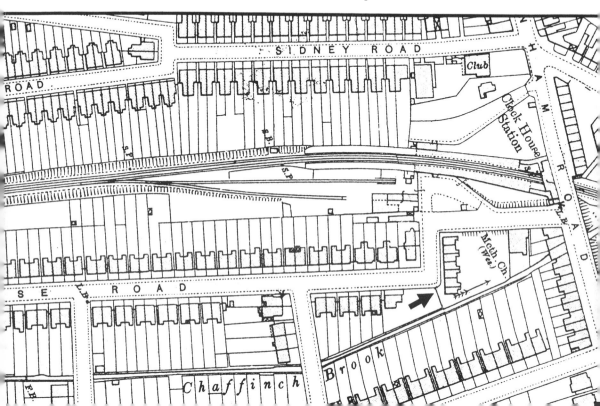

60. As at most suburban stations the goods yard was used mainly for coal inward. The yard is seen in 1953 and closed on 19th April 1965. The box was taken out of use on 19th August 1962. (British Rail)

61. There was no crossover; the yard was served by southbound trains. Class E1 no. 31165 is seen yet again, this time working the 1.55pm Wateringbury to London Bridge train on 2nd October 1954. This was a return hop pickers special. (D.Cullum)

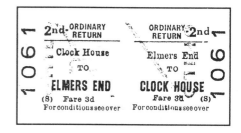

0020
SOUTHERN RAILWAY.
Special Arrangement
Available as advertised.
Aldershot to
ELMERS END
Third Class
FOR CONDITIONS
SEE BACK.
SOUTHERN RAILWAY.
Special Arrangement
Available as advertised.
Elmers End
Aldershot
Elmers End to
ALDERSHOT
Third Class
0020

2nd-ORDINARY RETURN | ORDINARY RETURN 2nd-
Clock House | Elmers End
TO | TO
ELMERS END | CLOCK HOUSE
(S) Fare 3d | Fare 3d (S)
For conditions see over | For conditions see over
1061 | 1061

2nd - SINGLE | SINGLE - 2nd
Lower Sydenham to
Lower Sydenham | Lower Sydenham
Clock House | Clock House
CLOCK HOUSE
(S) | (S)
9d Fare 9d
9026 | 9026
For conditions see over | For conditions see over

62. Clock House up starter and New Beckenham distant are seen in October 1961. All the station offices are on the bridge above. The track dips down at 1 in 100 on the 31 chain curve beyond the bridge, is level through the station and climbs at 1 in 200 most of the way to Elmers End. (J.Scrace)

63. Flooding has been a regular feature of life on the line. For many years an emergency timetable showed a 20 minute interval steam operated service of three coaches between Lower Sydenham and Addiscombe. This is the method of working on 1st June 1964, the class 33 locomotive being protected by plastic casings. (P.F.Sumner)

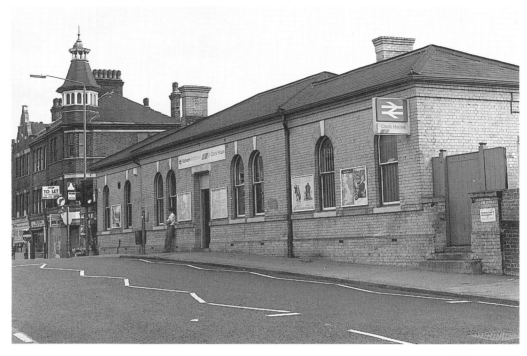

64. The exterior has changed little over the years and was recorded in August 1992. The original "Clock House" was opposite the buildings on the left on a site now occupied by educational establishments. (J.Scrace)

65. The up platform canopy was cut back as shown and that on the down side was removed in 1981. No.5446 is forming the 13.23 Charing Cross to Hayes on 25th August 1992. Most of these EPBs were to disappear by the end of the following year. (J.Scrace)

ELMERS END

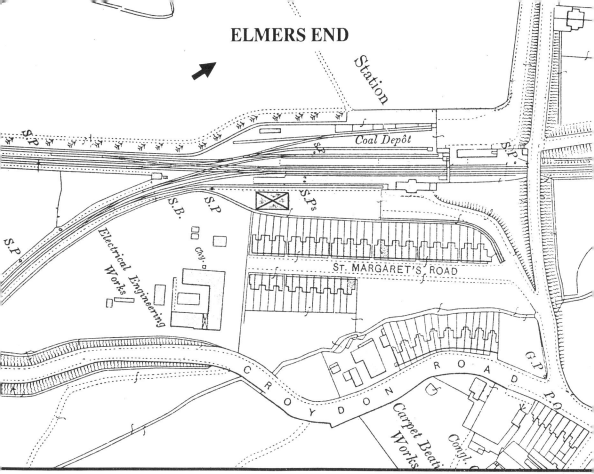

The station opened with the line on 1st April 1864 and was then the only intermediate stop on the new section between New Beckenham and Addiscombe. This is the arrangement in 1913.

66. This is the approach to the down side which was photographed from the bridge over Chaffinch Brook. (British Rail)

67. The up side exterior had become particularly shabby when recorded in the 1950s. (British Rail)

68. A train arrives from Hayes on 31st July 1954, the two dots indicating Charing Cross via the Ladywell Loop. Trains via Lewisham carried a bar in place of the dots. Cannon Street via Lewisham was a plain "H" but via the loop it carried a single dot. (R.C.Riley)

69. A 4EPB unit leaves the up bay, incorrectly showing a headcode, while another train arrives from Hayes on the 13-chain curve, which has a 20mph speed limit.
(A.J.Pike/F.Hornby)

70. Track alterations are in progress on 9th December 1956. These resulted in the through lines to Addiscombe being moved behind the signal box. Compare picture 69 with 73. The station suffered direct hits in three air raids in 1941, hence the gap in the canopy.
(Pamlin Prints)

71. An up train leaves in 1956 and gives us an opportunity to see the coal yard, which remained in use until 6th May 1963. Coal handling in those days was very labour intensive - shovels, bags and a flight of steps, visible on the left. (A.J.Pike/F.Hornby)

72. A photograph from October 1961 shows a new down side canopy nearing completion. It was photographed from the 1957 platform extension for 10-car trains. The up bay starting signal is for down Addiscombe trains. The up bay was relegated to an engineers siding on 27th September 1975. (J.Scrace)

73. The rerouting of the Addiscombe lines behind the box allowed the through platforms to be extended. Track alterations in 1947 included removal of the connection from the Hayes branch to the up bay and the reversal of the trailing crossover on the branch, so that up trains from Hayes could enter the down bay - left. This 1969 view features the box which closed on 27th September 1975. (J.Scrace)

74. A 1992 photograph shows the down bay devoid of track and that the colour light signalling presented the Hayes route as the main line. The building on the right dates from the commencement of electrification when it housed rotary convertors - AC motors coupled to DC generators which provided traction current. (M.Turvey)

76. Photographed on the same day is the Addiscombe 2-coach shuttle in the up bay (left). A London bound train waits alongside. Work had started on the rebuilding of the road bridge with a longer span which would permit platform lengthening at the north end. This was undertaken in 1993, along with the moving of the crossover northwards. (J.Scrace)

75. The buildings seen in picture 68 were severely damaged by fire on 16th December 1973 and were replaced by this object, recorded on 25th August 1992. The timetable showed some late afternoon services originating here, the stock having run empty from Addiscombe. (J.Scrace)

Hayes Branch
EDEN PARK

77. The branch was of dubious commercial value before the advent of large scale residential development of the area in the 1920s. Major improvments here prior to electrification included a new roof on the up side building (together with a new canopy) and extension of the down platform. The building had been damaged by fire.
(H.J.Patterson Rutherford)

The 1909 map indicates the country location of the station. From 1925 to 1934 ordinary tickets issued rose from 8000 to 75000, while season tickets increased from 61 to 4188.

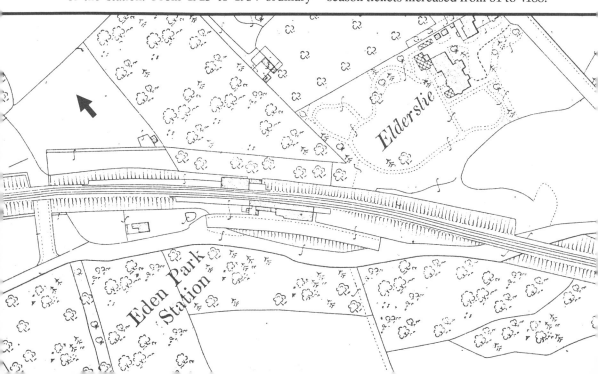

78. A subway gave access from the north side and also linked the platforms. This view from the 1950s shows the SR style notice board. A trailing siding from the up line, west of the station, and nearly one mile long, was in use in 1929-30 to convey materials for the construction of Monks Orchard (Bethlem Royal) Hospital in Shirley. (British Rail)

79. Looking towards Elmers End in 1960 we can observe the new concrete fence of the recent platform extension. Until 1899 there was a signal box at the Hayes end of the station, an over generous provision. The station is on a 1 in 89 gradient up from Elmers End, easing to 1 in 834 towards West Wickham. (Pamlin Prints)

80. Two photographs from 1991 emphasise that the station retains a rural ambience. The footpath to the up platform is adjacent to the flower bed on the right. Not only was the garden a joy to behold, but pot plants adorned the waiting room. (J.Scrace)

81. Still retaining its blue and grey livery, unit no. 5266 pauses to allow passengers to alight from the 12.23 from Charing Cross. In the early morning some school children board trains at this platform. (J.Scrace)

WEST WICKHAM

82. Tickets issued rose from 47000 in 1925 to 251000 in 1934, the figures for seasons being 336 and 18711 respectively. The goods yard is on the right of this photograph taken from the road bridge which appears on the right of the next map. (D.Cullum coll.)

83. This is the view west shortly before electrification; it includes the signal box which closed on 27th September 1975. There was road access to both platforms.
(H.J.Patterson-Rutherford)

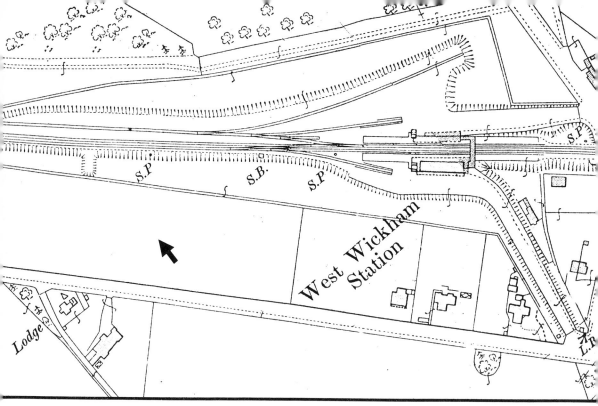

The 1909 survey reveals that the station was provided with end loading docks. These could have been used for the horse-drawn carriages of the gentry, an important traffic in earlier years.

84. A C class 0-6-0 shunts the yard in January 1954 as a first generation EMU approaches the down platform. Unlike the unit in the cover picture, this had been lengthened from three to four cars using a matching trailer. (A.J.Pike/F.Hornby)

85. The station suffered blast damage when a bomb fell between the platforms in May 1941. This is the replacement building on the up side, photographed in 1991. (J.Scrace)

86. A June 1992 picture shows posts ready to receive CCTV monitors for use with driver only operation (DOO) trains. A fourth rail to improve the return current path is provided on much of the branch. Here its position changes. It also appears in pictures 79, 81, 84 and 88. (F.Hornby)

HAYES

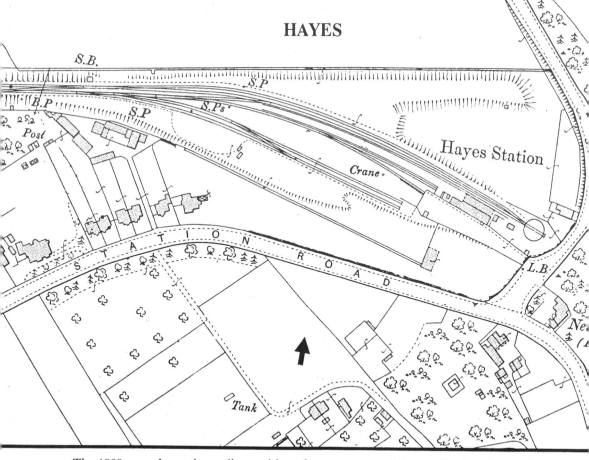

The 1909 map shows the earlier position of the signal box (S.B.) which had 17 levers. The part of the southern siding between the siding crossover and the up line had been added in 1899.

87. Initially the station had only one platform but the one on the right was added later. The chimneys of the station master's house flank that of the O class 0-6-0. The line climbs at 1 in 409 from West Wickham except for the section seen in the next picture, where it falls at 1 in 140. (D.Cullum coll.)

88. H class no. 324 approaches the terminus on 20th February 1926. The service on the branch had been partially operated by electric trains since the previous September, mainly for driver training. The bridge is reported to have once carried a footpath and subsequently the garden of a nearby house. (H.C.Casserley)

By the time of this 1936 survey, housing had engulfed the area and every aspect of the station had been altered. The yard crane had a capacity of 7 tons. Freight facilities were withdrawn on 19th April 1965 but the sidings were retained by the engineers until January 1971.

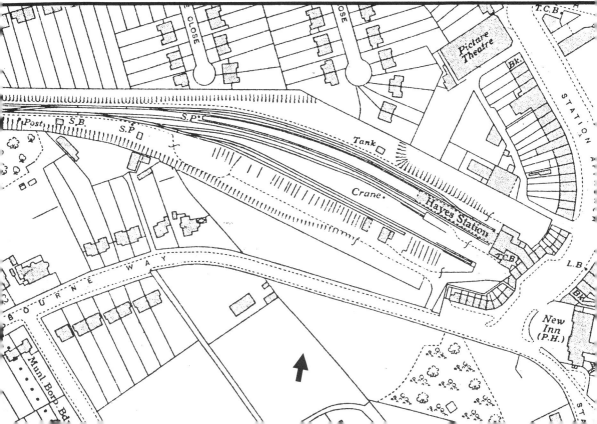

89. Photographed between 1925 and 1935, the loop on the left became a siding in 1969 and was later removed. The two coaches on the right were probably attached to a 3SUB unit. Such trailers were run between pairs of units at peak times until September 1948. (D.Cullum coll.)

90. An entirely new station was completed in 1935 in response to dramatic increases in the number of tickets issued. The 1925 and 1934 figures were 1000 and 177000 respectively, with seasons at 159 and 5831. (British Rail)

DOWN		
12.25am		Bricklayers Arms to Lower Sydenham
12.20am		North End Sidings to Lower Sydenham
1.45am		North End Sidings to Lower Sydenham
3.17am		Bricklayers Arms to Addiscombe (due 5.20am)
2.50am		North End Sidings to Lower Sydenham
4.07am		Bricklayers Arms to Hayes (due 5.49am)
5.15am		Catford Bridge to Beckenham Junction
6.20am		Elmers End to Sanderstead
11.30pm		North End Sidings to Lower Sydenham
UP		
12.45am		Lower Sydenham to North End Sidings
12.50am		Addiscombe to Bricklayers Arms (due 4.20am)
2.20am		Lower Sydenham to Hither Green
2.50am		Lower Sydenham to North End Sidings
6.36am		Hayes to West Wickham
10.01pm	SO	Hayes to Elmers End
11.50pm	SX	Hayes to Bricklayers Arms (due 2.05am)
12.00mgt		Beckenham Junction to Catford Bridge

Typical freight timetable in the 1930s.

91. The arcade between the concourse and the entrance was flanked by small shops, one of which was occupied in 1993 by a hairdressing business named "Railway Cuttings". This view from the 1950s includes the regulation stretcher cupboard. (British Rail)

92. Small yellow warning panels had appeared on the trains but the clock still required winding and departure notices needed chalk. By 1993 all these features had gone but the lattice gates remained, having long disappeared from the main London termini. (British Rail)

93. The 33-lever signal box was in use until 27th September 1975, three weeks after this photograph was taken. Control of the branch was thereafter from the London Bridge panel. (J.Scrace)

94. The entrance was badly damaged by bombing on 15th September 1940, repairs not being completed until 1956. This 1983 view shows that the original SR profile was not restored. Ten years later there was still no nameboard on the building. (F.Hornby)

95. The 12.08 to Charing Cross was recorded on 5th July 1991 at which time there were still facing and trailing crossovers beyond the platform end. The inevitable car parks flanked the station. (J.Scrace)

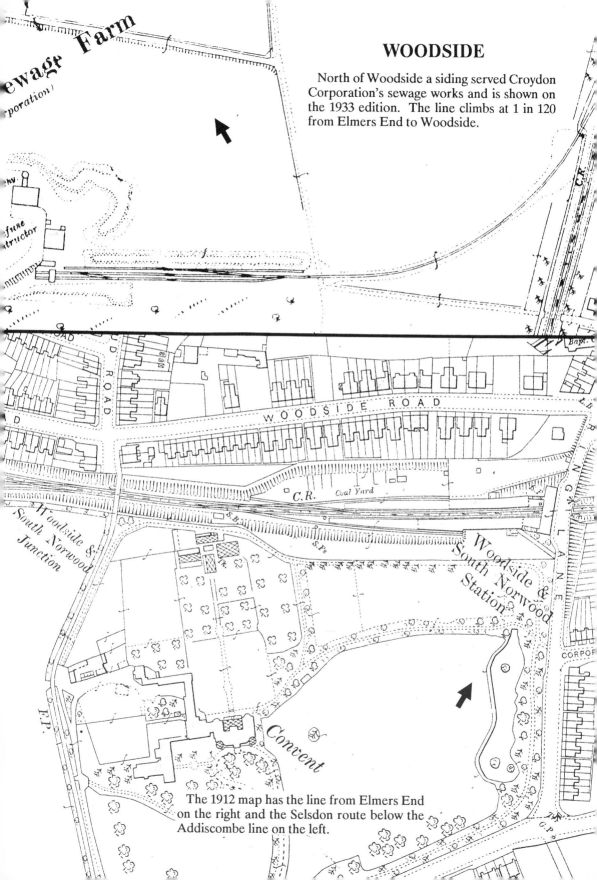

WOODSIDE

North of Woodside a siding served Croydon Corporation's sewage works and is shown on the 1933 edition. The line climbs at 1 in 120 from Elmers End to Woodside.

The 1912 map has the line from Elmers End on the right and the Selsdon route below the Addiscombe line on the left.

96. The station opened in 1871 and became a junction on 10th August 1885 when the joint line to Selsdon (Road) opened. An LBSCR "Terrier" 0-6-0T waits in the down bay with a train of four-wheelers.
(G.Metherall/D.Cullum)

97. The 2.42pm Cannon Street to Addiscombe was photographed at Woodside one week before electric services were introduced in 1926. The locomotive is Q1 class no. A363, ex-SER and withdrawn later that year.
(H.C.Casserley)

98. The down line to Selsdon is barred with a banner as a class C2X 0-6-0 with an engineers train passes during electrification work in 1935. The Addiscombe line passes under the bridge on the right. (Lens of Sutton)

99. The station was officially "Woodside and South Norwood" between 1st October 1908 and 2nd October 1944. This is the prospective passenger's perspective in the 1950s. (Lens of Sutton)

→

100. A northward panorama in October 1955 includes an Addiscombe train devoid of headcode, a perforated concrete signal post and the full extent of the coal yard. The sidings had been added in 1878, a signal box having been erected the previous year. (Pamlin Prints)

101. Concrete posts were widely used on the SECR but not elsewhere. The tapered posts on the brackets were of wood. The junction is beyond the bridge which carried only a footpath. (Pamlin Prints)

102. Four former running rails replaced the concrete post and lattice structures of LSWR style (seen in the foreground of picture 100) replaced the wood. Seen in 1969 the well groomed box was functioning until 24th June 1984, over a year after it ceased to control a junction. (J.Scrace)

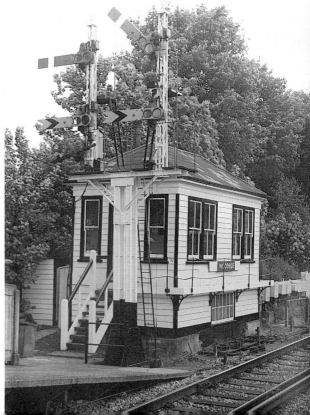

103. The goods yard closed on 30th September 1963, facilitating the extension of the up platform as shown. In the 1930s freight trains were largely nocturnal, as indicated in the table by picture no. 90. (Lens of Sutton)

104. The last day of operation to Selsdon was 13th May 1983. Unit 5763 is seen working the 17.12 Sanderstead to Elmers End on that day. In the background is St.Johns Lane bridge where the 1 in 300 climb to Addiscombe starts. (J.Scrace)

105. The 17.30 Elmers End to Sanderstead is on the right on the last day of operation of the Selsdon route. On the left is the 17.31 Addiscombe to Elmers End shuttle. The Croydon Tramlink proposal envisages relaying lines on the right, abandonment of those on the left and provision of a stop near the bridge, which carries Blackhorse Lane. (J.Scrace)

106. On 25th August 1992 the station was in good order, complete with windbreak. By 1993 the windows were boarded up and the station had become the first on the route to be totally unstaffed. (J.Scrace)

ADDISCOMBE

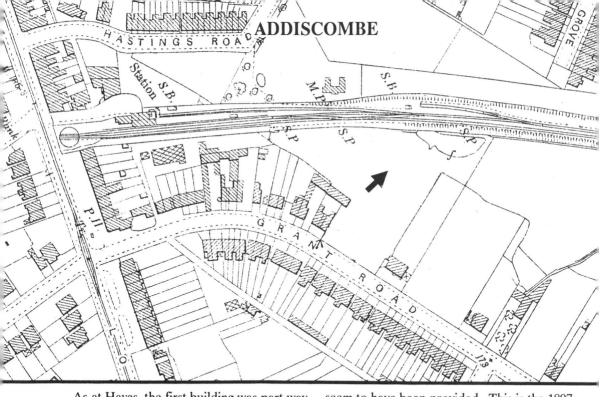

As at Hayes, the first building was part way down the platform, the turntable saved a point at the end of the line but no goods facilities seem to have been provided. This is the 1897 map.

The 1910 edition shows the revised position of the turntable; the long siding to the right of it was added in 1903.

107. The East India Company's Military College was sold in 1862 and Mr Addiscombe Thorne soon started to build villas in the grounds. The modest first station was replaced by this substantial red brick structure in 1899. Opened as "Addiscombe Road", it became "Croydon (Addiscombe)" and then "Addiscombe (Croydon)" in 1926, the suffix being finally dropped in 1955. (Lens of Sutton)

SOUTHERN RAILWAY.
Available DAY of Issue ONLY. (SEE BACK)
Addiscombe Road to
ELMER'S END
3d   Third Class   3d
E   s End   Elmer's End

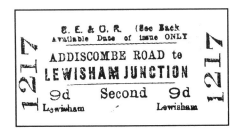

E. E. & C. R. (See Back
Available Date of Issue ONLY
ADDISCOMBE ROAD to
LEWISHAM JUNCTION
9d   Second   9d
Lewisham   Lewisham

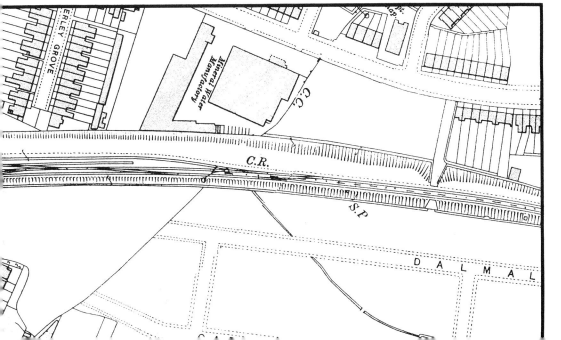

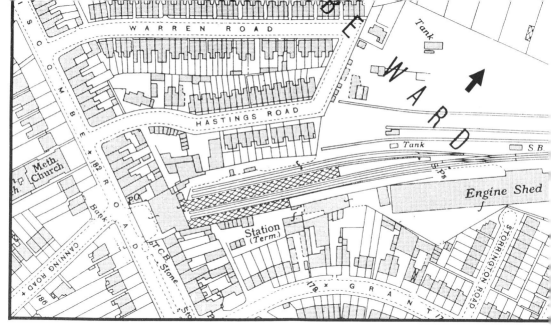

108. Imposing gate pillars, surmounted by tapered lanterns, terminated the ornate railings. Outside was a passing loop in the tramway, which ran to Addiscombe from 1st January 1902. (Lens of Sutton)

S. E. & C. R. (SEE BACK
Available Day of issue ONLY.

ADDISCOMBE ROAD to

CLOCK HOUSE

4d Second Class 4d

Clock House   Clock House

2690   2690

Addiscombe Station

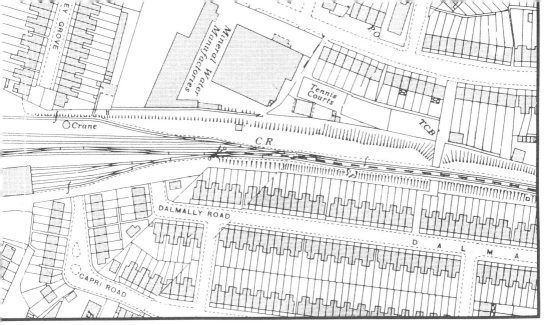

The 1941 revision has the 1925 carriage shed marked as *Engine Shed*. Also added since the previous edition is the goods yard, which was provided with a 5-ton crane.

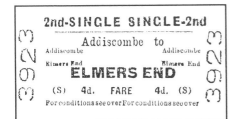

109. A 3-car EMU runs into platform 2 past the crowded coal yard while a steam locomotive stands outside the electric train shed. Centre is a typical SECR water valve wheel; the water column was retained primarily for goods locomotives but also for the regular flood emergency service. (Lens of Sutton)

110. Steam stock is berthed in the "Bay siding", which is seen from platform 3. This platform was removed in 1957 to make way for an additional berthing siding. Several proposals were made to terminate Metropolitan trains here instead of New Cross and a trial clearance train ran unsuccessfully on 17th February 1926. (Lens of Sutton)

112. A view in the opposite direction on the same day includes first and second generation stock. The last 4 SUB (right) was withdrawn on 1st October 1983. The succeeding class of EPBs (later numbered 415/6) were being replaced by Networker class 465 units in 1993. (British Rail)

←————————

111. A 4SUB stands at platform 1 on 29th September 1950, by which time the coal yard was not very busy. Note that the adjacent berthing siding was not electrified. (British Rail)

113. The wooden floored 1988 booking hall retained many of its original features in the 1960s and still did so as it entered the 1990s. By 1993 the booking office was staffed on weekday mornings only. (British Rail)

114. The shuttle to Elmers End was being worked by 2EPB no. 5753 on 5th June 1969. Freight services had been withdrawn on 17th June 1968 but the sidings remained usable until November 1969. (J.Scrace)

115. The branch shuttle has been traditionally operated from platform 2 (right), no. 1 generally berthing stock outside the peak hours. The platform canopies date from 1896. Within 100 years, they and the entire station could become redundant if trams operate over part of the route. (C.Hall)

116. Although it had lost its fine boundary features, the building was still a pure unaltered SER design, although completed in the first months of the existence of the SECR. It was recorded in the 1970s when its future still seemed secure. (C.Hall)

117. Unit no. 6236 departs for Elmers End at 13.08 on 16th August 1986 and passes the 38-lever signal box. Eleven levers were out of use - it had 47 at its optimum. On the left is the 1957 berthing siding. (J.Scrace)

118. Platform lengthening in 1957 resulted in
no. 1 road being moved behind the box -
compare with picture 111. Leaving from it on
16th August 1986 is the Rank Xerox Exhibition
train. (J.Scrace)

S E & C R   SEE BACK.
Available Day of Issue ONLY
ADDISCOMBE ROAD to
CHARING CROSS
1/2 Second Class 1/2
Charing X.   Charing X.
4631   4631

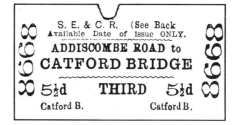

S. E. & C. R.   (See Back
Available Date of Issue ONLY.
ADDISCOMBE ROAD to
CATFORD BRIDGE
5½d   THIRD   5½d
Catford B.   Catford B.
8668   8668

119. Drivers ceased to book on here on 12th April 1993 although berthing of up to six trains continued, as witnessed earlier on 15th July 1992. It became the last location of mechanical signalling in the London area as the station awaited its fate. Networker trains would not be berthed here. (M.Turvey)

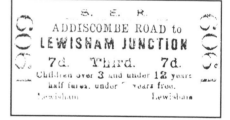

2486
SOUTHERN RAILWAY.
CHEAP DAY
Available as advertised.
Addiscombe to
CLOCK HOUSE,
EDEN PK. ELMERS END
or NEW BECKENHAM
(Issued at Elmer's End.)
Third Class
FOR CONDITIONS SEE BACK
SOUTHERN RAILWAY.
CHEAP DAY
Available as advertised.
Elmers End to
ADDISCOMBE
Third Class
2486

S. E. R.
ADDISCOMBE ROAD to
LEWISHAM JUNCTION
7d. Third. 7d.
Children over 3 and under 12 years
half fares, under 3 years free.
Lewisham   Lewisham

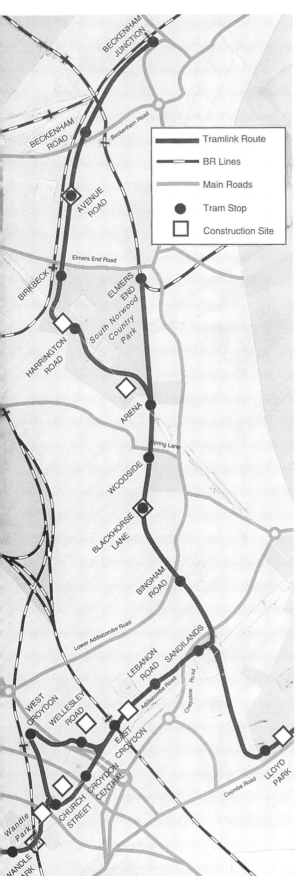

CROYDON TRAMLINK

In 1993 a bill was before Parliament for the construction of Croydon Tramlink, which would link Wimbledon with Beckenham and replace BR trains between Wimbledon and West Croydon. Promoted jointly by London Transport and the London Borough of Croydon, a triangular route around the periphery of the shopping centre was proposed with street-running eastwards to link up the former Woodside - Selsdon BR route, closed in 1982. A branch southward would continue to New Addington while a northward route would use the existing BR route between Blackhorse Lane and Elmers End. The Birkbeck - Beckenham Junction section would run alongside the BR track. Tram stops on the Wimbledon route are shown below picture 103 in our *Mitcham Junction Lines* album.

120. A simulation of George Street in the future shows one of the proposed three-car articulated trams proceeding from Croydon Central towards the triangular junction and East Croydon station. A similar system that opened in Manchester in April 1992 carried 7 million passengers in its first year and so there was optimism that Tramlink would help relieve the chronic road traffic congestion of the Croydon area. (Dept. of Planning & Transportation, London Borough of Croydon)

Map legend

- Tramlink Route
- BR Lines
- Main Roads
- ● Tram Stop
- ▢ Construction Site

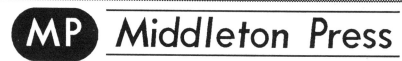

MP Middleton Press

Easebourne Lane, Midhurst. West Sussex. GU29 9AZ   Tel: (0730) 813169 Fax: (0730) 812601
..... Write or telephone for our latest list .....

BRANCH LINES

Branch Line to Allhallows
Branch Lines to Alton
Branch Lines tround Ascot
Branch Lines to East Grinstead
Branch Lines tround Effingham Jn
Branch Lines to Exmouth
Branch Line to Fairford
Branch Lines around Gosport
Branch Line to Hawkhurst
Branch Line to Hayling
Branch Lines to Horsham
Branch Lines around Huntingdon
Branch Lines to Longmoor
Branch Line to Lyme Regis
Branch Line to Lynton
Branch Lines around March
Branch Lines around Midhurst
Branch Line to Minehead
Branch Lines to Newport
Branch Lines around Portmadoc (1923-46)
Branch Lines to Seaton & Sidmouth
Branch Line to Selsey
Branch Lines around Sheerness
Branch Line to Shrewsbury
Branch Line to Southwold
Branch Line to Swanage
Branch Line to Tenterden
Branch Lines to Tunbridge Wells
Branch Lines tround Weymouth
Branch Lines around Wimborne

LONDON SUBURBAN RAILWAYS

Charing Cross to Dartford
Crystal Palace and Catford Loop
Holborn Viaduct to Lewisham
Kingston and Hounslow Loops
Lewisham to Dartford
London Bridge to Addiscombe
Mitcham Junction Lines
West Croydon to Epsom

STEAMING THROUGH

Steaming through East Hants
Steaming through the Isle of Wight
Steaming through Surrey
Steaming through West Hants
Steaming through West Sussex

SOUTH COAST RAILWAYS

Ashford to Dover
Bournemouth to Weymouth
Brighton to Eastbourne
Brighton to Worthing
Chichester to Portsmouth
Dover to Ramsgate
Eastbourne to Hastings
Hastings to Ashford
Southampton to Bournemouth

SOUTHERN MAIN LINES

Basingstoke to Salisbury
Charing Cross to Orpington
Crawley to Littlehampton
East Croydon to Three Bridges
Epsom to Horsham
Exeter to Barnstaple
Faversham to Dover
Haywards Heath to Seaford
London Bridge to East Croydon
Orpington to Tonbridge
Salisbury to Yeovil
Sittingbourne to Ramsgate
Three Bridges to Brighton
Tonbridge to Hastings
Victoria to Bromley South
Victoria to East Croydon
Waterloo to Windsor
Waterloo to Woking
Woking to Southampton
Yeovil to Exeter

COUNTRY RAILWAY ROUTES

Andover to Southampton
Bath To Evercreech Junction
Bournemouth to Evercreech Jn
Burnham to Evercreech Junction
East Kent Light Railway
Fareham to Salisbury
Guildford to Redhill
Reading to Guildford
Redhill to Ashford
Strood to Paddock Wood
Woking to Alton
Yeovil to Dorchester

TRAMWAY CLASSICS

Brighton's Tramways
Greenwich and Dartford Tramways
Hastings Tramways
Thanet's Tramways

BUS BOOKS

Eastbourne Bus Story
Tillingbourne Bus Story

OTHER RAILWAY BOOKS

Garraway Father & Son
Industrial Railways of the South East
London Chatham & Dover Railway
South Eastern Railway
West Sussex Railways in the 1980s

MILITARY BOOKS

Battle Over Portsmouth
Battle Over Sussex 1940
Military Defence of West Sussex

WATERWAY ALBUMS

Hampshire Waterways
Kent and East Sussex Waterways
Surrey Waterways

COUNTRY BOOKS

Betwixt Petersfield and Midhurst
Brickmaking in Sussex
East Grinstead Then and Now
Leigh Park
Walking Ashdown Forest